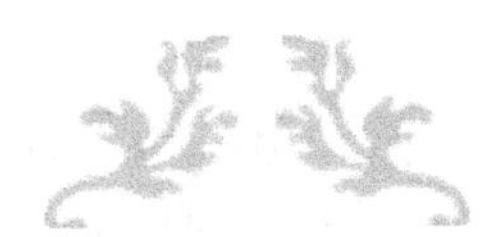

DEPRESSED TO
SUCCESS

THE ONLY MANUAL YOU WILL EVER NEED

VANESSA VANITA

Quantity sales special discounts are available on quantity purchases by corporations, associations, and others. For details, contact the publisher at the address above.

Orders by U.S. trade bookstores and wholesalers. Email info@ BeyondPublishing.net

The Beyond Publishing Speakers Bureau can bring authors to your live event. For more information or to book an event contact the Beyond Publishing Speakers Bureau speak@BeyondPublishing.net

The Author can be reached directly @ VanessaVanita.com

Manufactured and printed in the United States of America distributed globally by BeyondPublishing.net

New York | Los Angeles | London | Sydney

ISBN Hardcover: 978-1-949873-56-6

ISBN Softcover: 9-78-1-952884-02-3

CONTENTS

I stopped writing a long time ago

Writing for me was always a choice against living, I never seemed to be able to do both - write and live at the same time. In the past few years I have lived lots of life, and I was scared to go back to these places, scared to open these doors, scared to walk down these steps into myself.

The reason I am writing again, and the reason I am writing to you now, is for the sole purpose of trying to reach you - of reaching out to you - because I know where you are, and the only way to get to where you are and pull you out is by writing to you. That is why I am here, why I am digging into myself until my heart bleeds again, scratching on old wounds, removing scab, feeling my scars. This is not me writing from a place far away. I didn't "make it", I didn't overcome, I didn't fully heal or find a cure. *But* I have found a path. And I can be your guide. It won't be easy, this path is dimly lit and rocky and winding and there will be crossroads and obstacles along the way, and the journey will be lifelong - BUT, and I make this promise here to you: It will become brighter and brighter if you just keep going forward, no matter how tired, no matter how weak, no matter how desperately you wanna turn back around and stay in comfortable old pain.

I have lived in comfortable pain mud for 3 decades. Stuck. So stuck, with my hands and feet, immovable. I have been to these muddy places over and over again, more than I wanna admit, longer than anyone should. Have you heard of my favorite book by German author Michael Ende? It is called "The Neverending Story". Do you remember how Atreyu's horse Artax was sinking into the Swamp of Sadness. Atreyu and Artax were one and the same. Artax was the tortured soul that desperately wanted to leave life, to be free of pain, to drown in depression. Atreyu was the warrior, the fighter for new life. He tries to help Artax, tries to take his old painful past with him, but the mud is too deep and he is not strong enough, he has to watch his horse die and immediately has to make the decision not to die with it, to fight himself out of the swamp. He has to decide if he wants to live. In a moment where there is nothing left but an overwhelming sense of despair, nothing left of his old self, when everything seemed to come to an end, Atreyu fights himself out of the swamp.

Years ago, when there was nothing left of me, I made a similar decision. I made the decision to start from nothing, to start right from where I was. From the mud, from the mess, the dirt, the swamp I was in. I started at the end of me. It wasn't rock bottom, or a conscious decision to change my life or to finally be free of pain. When you are feeling this lifeless, you don't dream of being free of emotional pain because you cannot imagine life without it. You don't know any different. What changed everything for me, was the moment that I allowed myself to be nothing for once. To be gone, to be without "self". No expectations, no masks, no identity, no promises. And slowly my nothing self was able to feel itself through the pain, hurt from all its injuries, no running, no numbing, no pretending, no hiding. Pain by Pain by Pain. And piece by piece, parts of something new appeared, something of substance, a strong mental framework. I was put together in a way I never was before.

Do you remember when Bastian Balthasar Bux had used up all his memories and had to start from Nothingness to created Fantasia new? (This is the moment where I wish I would write this book in German, my first language, since "Die Unendliche Geschichte" is a German book and and deserves to be referenced in its original language, and Fantasia is really Phantasien and that's important. This is when I realize, dear Reader, that there is a reason I am not writing my book in German. And that it would have never been written if I would have to do so in my native language. It's the language I feel my pain in. So I'm writing this in English - I apologize to Michael Ende: Fantasia it is for now).

My healing started when I was accepting me being Nothing, and I began building a foundation from there. But not from memories - just like Bastian I was not allowed to use those anymore: past memories would not built my new life. I had to build something entirely new, armed with a beating heart that had been beating this entire time for me without being appreciated, and I started appreciating that it was beating, and I was humbled when I realized that it had never stopped despite me trying my hardest to break it. I was humbled by my body, humbled by my lungs, my skin, my brain. They had never given up on me. And I slowly started repaying them by giving support, by going straight through my trauma, my shame, the disapproval. I started changing what I fed that body that I had abandoned, I stopped starving it, abusing it and talking down on it. I started giving my lungs so much fresh air that it was at all times flooded with oxygen and constantly spat out new ideas to heal. I started seeing people the way I could now see myself: as naked, flawed, human. No matter what gender, what status, what ideology, I could see myself in them. I accepted others because I started accepting myself and I started trusting others because I could suddenly trust myself. I trusted myself enough that I started moving away from things and people that were not meant for me. Not in every waking moment, but enough for me to build on that.

Let me be your Atreyu for now. We are one and the same, there is no difference between us, except for me having more strength right now to pull, because I am not sinking anymore. Please grab my hand and hold on to it, and let me pull you out of this swamp just enough, just to hold you for now so you don't sink further, and maybe you start wiggling your feet, and maybe, while I don't let go of your hand, you make the decision that you don't want to sink, that you have some strength left in you.

Maybe you can feel your heart beating. Maybe you take a deep breath and feel your lungs pumping air, your body is working to keep you alive. It's all yours, it's not going to give up, not in this moment. Your body, no matter how sick it might be, is waiting for you to support it. Don't give up on it. And if you need me to hold your hand for now, I'll do that. Picture and feel me holding your hand while you read the chapters of this book that I am only writing hoping that you make the decision that you want to live! Because writing this hurts me just as much as it hurts you reading this. We are connected, you are reading the words while I am holding your hand. Don't let go. Now let's get out of here.

CHAPTER 1

Inner Child Rescue

I remember being in the lady foot locker dressing room of a random mall in Florida, with my Dad peeking in to check out some kind of workout gear I had tried on, consisting of black Nike biker shorts and a sports bra, in the attempt to show him my motivation to stop being an embarrassment and a lazy piece of shit and to finally get in shape. I was about 11. My Dad looked me up and down, grimaced and said: "This kind of stuff is not meant for your body type, you are built like a speed skater, women are supposed to look like an hourglass, you instead look like a Christmas tree" pointing to my thighs in the tight spandex, "you've got to work on that."

The fact that I still remember this moment like it was yesterday, is funny to me, since my dad was a professional body shamer, not just towards me, but towards himself and everyone around him, so that there were countless of these painful assassinations of my vulnerable children's soul that I could remember, but some of them seemed to have hurt deeper than others. I would still hear his voice a few years ago whenever I felt fat in a certain outfit or would see an unflattering photo of myself, or whatever my body dysmorphia would sell me as unflattering. I also remember him making fun of my growing breasts, forbidding me to talk about my period in front of my friends and shamed me about not being able to use tampons when I first started menstruating at the age of 12. I was using pads and could not go swimming - for some reason the fact that I did not want to shove a bleached piece of cotton into my vagina seemed to infuriate him. Certain things you will never forget, no matter how much inner child work you do, no matter how far you come in your healing.

Having a father who seemingly resented me for existing, for having a body that was too much, a voice that was too loud, a mind that was too precautious, and a soul that could see right through him, resulted in me living in a constant state of fear from my earliest memories on. He was verbally abusive towards me, and I was addicted to his abuse and tried my hardest to somehow either escape his rage or win his approval, simultaneously. I would never be successful.

My extraordinary mother, one of the most loving and kind people you could ever meet, managed to shield us as kids from a lot of my father's anger. If there is someone living in your home, that is supposed to love and protect you, and instead rejects and insults you, whose voice and fury and disapproval you fear more than anything, who makes you feel worthless before you even know what worth means and small, before you have a chance to grow, and who in any given moment could erupt and destroy every last bit of peace and hope within yourself, then your little life becomes a war zone. You will begin living in a state of chronic stress, that in my case led to chronic inflammation, physical illness, depression, social anxiety, disordered eating, suicidal thoughts.

From the outside it seemed like I had everything a kid could wish for. On the inside, I was living in emotional poverty. My thoughts evolved around shame, self-hatred, self-harm and insecurities. I was bullied at home and the bullying would continue in school. I was extremely shy, painfully introverted, socially awkward and full of self-loathing. I always describe my childhood and adolescence as living behind a glass wall. I saw the world outside going on, but I could not participate, being stuck in deep emotional suffering. I don't believe that my father alone was to blame for me being as introverted as I was, but I do believe his abuse mixed with my sensitivity and emotionality created a toxic cocktail that functioned as the base for decades of self-harm that would be following. Here I want to use the opportunity to recommend a book that has changed my life forever and aided in my healing process more than anything else I ever read and I strongly believe it can be of great service in your own healing journey: "Complex PTSD : **From Surviving To Thriving by** Peter Walker."

I was traumatized, and if you picked up this book, chances are you might be suffering from your own trauma, often without being aware of it. My unprocessed trauma kept me in a cycle of depression, shame, self-loathing that I could not find my way out of until I was well into adulthood. I wish someone back then had realized what I was suffering from, and that I would have been able to open up to people, and to get the help I needed to heal. Being traumatized ironically comes with the need to cover up your true emotions, so most of us suffer in silence, some of us their entire lives. This is why I am writing this book. I am not a therapist, psychologist or philosopher. But I have been where you are, and I can use my voice to tell you about my way out.

CHAPTER 2

Wash Your Brain

We wash all parts of our bodies regularly, we are taught from an early age to constantly wash our hands, brush our teeth, scrub our ears. When the real danger are not just the germs on our hands. The real dirt, the grime that can build up and pollute every part of our brains, those toxic waste thoughts, that make you see and believe things about yourself that are not real, and even if they were real, need to be addressed and recycled. The part of us that is in urgent need of constant upkeep and cleansing and exfoliating, is our mind. And no one teaches you that.

I grew up in Berlin, Germany. A place of abundance, one of the richest countries in the world, a place with a doctor on every street corner, with great schools, a welfare system, health care. The people, teachers, grown ups that shaped me were for the most part good, educated people, that expected a lot from adolescents. We were expected to be driven, ambitious and down to earth. Save our money, be humble, don't dream too big, stay with our feet on the ground, be disciplined and strict with ourselves. Education and culture were higher valued than material things, bragging about wealth was considered tacky. We are a culture of debating, writing, questioning the status quo, all this is ingrained in my generation.

I will never understand how as a society that is so aware, so educated, so progressive, we fail to address the number one thing that leads children down a path of self-destruction, that eventually creates suffering adults, who turn to drugs and alcohol to numb the unaddressed pain, that eventually have children they pass their trauma down to. Of course this problem is not a German one, but this is where I was raised, and even though I don't ever wanna move back, I have respect for the mentality of addressing your own bullshit and sorting things out, getting to the bottom of things, evoking change. I had to leave my country to appreciate this culture, the notion of authenticity and honesty with yourself and others. That said, I don't understand why a system so sophisticated fails to take real care of their children, why "mental health" is not its own subject in school, mandatory, through your entire school career. It makes me angry that we teach our kids to clean up after themselves, to wear fresh socks every morning, to look presentable, and how we fail to equip them with the tools that are actually needed to survive, to find yourself when you get lost, to allow yourself to create a life you want to live, a toolset to fight addiction, depression, to cope with pain. Because this is life. Pain and suffering cannot be avoided, and that is not the goal. The most important thing we need to teach children is how to cope with the lows, the self-doubts, the bullying, from yourself and others, the shame, the abuse if it occurs, the chaos in their homes, the fear of the future. How teachers will say, that it is important to endure adversity and social anxiety in order to build character, when no-one helps explaining how the mind works and how to deal with negative thoughts flooding a child's brain when it gets bullied, body shamed, excluded. We raise little soldiers but we don't arm them.

I wish someone would have taught me early on that negative self-talk, self-loathing, perfectionism, shame were nothing else but toxic waste, and would in fact not be useful tools in order to reach my goals, to become happier, prettier, thinner, smarter, more successful, more respected, finally loved. I thought if I just punished myself enough for my shortcomings, my constant failing, disciplining myself to the point of self-abuse, being as strict as possible, withholding love from myself until I was perfect - that all these things would eventually lead to relief, maybe happiness, maybe peace.

It took me more than 30 years to be able to acknowledge how wrong I was, how much time I wasted living in this polluted state of mind. There are a multitude of reasons why someone suffers from anxiety, depression, eating disorders, personality disorders. They are often but not always a consequence of trauma, sometimes it's simply your brain crying for help. There are many forms of therapy, there is medication, there are things you can do to cope. No matter the route we choose, there will never come a time that our brain does not create thoughts. As long as we live, as long as our brain functions properly, we will think thoughts. Nothing to stop them from coming, no use in fighting them. No matter what it is you choose to do to help you heal, to help you process, to help you through - toxic thoughts will come, inevitably, often times completely unexpected, always uninvited. The goal is not to eliminate them, because it is impossible. The goal is not eternal positivity. For many of us the term "think positive" sounds like fraud, and I am not writing this book to teach you some artificial mantras, and that's what affirmations are.

If it empowers you to tell yourself "I am beautiful", "I am worthy" to your mirror image in the morning, that's amazing. Positive affirmations work for you and reach you. They never reached me. What I had to figure out, and it was a dreadful process with many losses on the way, was how to exercise bad thoughts that were popping into my head, and how to stop them from multiplying and manifesting more pain, from making me quit my job, starving myself, ruining my life. It took me decades to realize that I had all the power within me to de-toxify my brain, to cleanse my mind. And when I was well into my healing journey, after my son was born, I realized that I had established a little system, a method, so easy it should be taught in kindergarten. It formed out of necessity, and it took shape because a healthy mindset grows and evolves, a toxic one stays stuck. Thoughts are so abstract, and often times it is too difficult to even express to yourself the confusion and the agony that is raging in your brain. So I had to make it really, really simple for myself, in order to survive bad episodes, in order to break out of a vicious cycle.

Here is my method, I do it many times a day, whenever I need it. It takes a little practice and you will feel silly at first, but I promise it works. And it will work in ways you can't foresee yet, because for every eliminated bad thought comes a positive one, you will become proud for taking control over your mind, and once you stop letting thoughts dictate what you do in a day, what you do with your life, the sky becomes the limit, and you realize the endless possibilities that are opening up to a mind that is steadfast and armed against intruders. The key is to do it no matter what state you are in, if it is a good day or bad day, a good or bad year, if you are feeling hopeless or hopeful. No matter what the status quo is, this method of thought control has to be mandatory and like tooth brushing: a daily lifelong routine, a no-brainer (see what I did there)

This is what you do

Every time a negative thought about yourself pops in your head, you imagine it as a bubble. Floating in your head completely out of the blue. As soon as you acknowledge that bubble, become aware of its presence - awareness is the most important aspect and the most difficult step in this - you will probably feel some kind of emotional pain, and you're allowed to feel it. However, as soon as you become aware of the nature of the bubble: toxic, useless, destructive, YOU POP IT. Immediately.

As fast as you can. Make it a game. How fast can you dismiss a negative thought about yourself? And here comes the part that will lead to your success if you can cultivate it: You do not let any negative thought about your self worth influence whatever you do! That moment, that day, that year. I know this might sounds very unusual or even rebellious to some of you who are used to living and are comfortable in a carefully curated toxic mindset that keeps them safe and shielded from any kind of new and possibly enlightening experiences. Change is so so scary, especially if you, like me lived a life behind glass, full of millions of bubbles that kept me from realizing that I deserve more, that I am strong enough to shatter that glass, that I can create myself new if I just learn to pop the bubbles and start to move. Having a set daily routine in place is crucial for the success of this silly little method, because it makes it way easier for you to stay on track and not get carried away, dwelling and indulging in old pain. Practice this method with small, not extremely triggering thoughts and when you get better in staying on track with your daily tasks, and you can feel becoming more productive and less manipulated by the bubbles, you can move on to the real stuff, the deep thoughts, and as you go on popping your bubbles so much freedom will set in, and you feel like you can fly some days, because the thing that kept you from reaching all the heights you were dreaming of reaching, your own mind will not have power over you anymore. No better: it will from now on serve you! You will use the power of your thoughts and start thinking better ones, more valuable ones, and you will start sharing them with the world, because it will feel like you unlocked a treasure box full of secrets that will relief suffering in others.

Please write me if you try this method and let me know how much it transformed your life, as I know it will.

I now teach my son every day to pop his bubbles, hoping that it will stay with him forever, long after I am gone to remind him how wonderful and beautiful and divine he is. And so are you.

CHAPTER 3

Stop Running

In the year 2008, I seemed dead set on killing myself. Coming out of one of the coldest and darkest winters ever, full of heartbreak, financial struggles, hopelessness, Spring and Summer came and I went into full on mania. I have not been diagnosed with bipolar disorder and I don't think I meet the criteria, but I did use to go through phases of extreme depression followed by weeks or months of hyperactivity and a state I would describe as sheer ecstasy. I could probably still go to these extreme places, but healthy eating, exercise, a set daily routine and self accountability to stay on track with my goals keep my in check and are a huge component in achieving a necessary balance in my life.

The ecstasy and high of my manic episodes would often be incredibly thrilling and I almost enjoyed the drama and chaos I created for myself. If you are riddled with depression from an early age on, you tend to look forward and crave those hyperactive episodes, they remind you that you're still alive, that there is a world behind the glass wall, that there is laughter and lighthearted fun and freedom. But I usually paid the price for all that freedom.

I was never a big drinker. Coming from a family where alcohol addiction was common, I always thought I had to be careful not to like it too much. One warm night in the Summer of 2008 I drank Vodka mixed with Champagne, my go to drink that year, a cheap cocktail mixed at the club I would go to several nights a week, miserable and lonely, surrounded by people catering to my destructive lifestyle. That cocktail was as toxic as the company I kept, and I only ordered it because I had noticed how it would make me extremely drunk, almost delirious and high, after just a few sips. That night I felt especially low, I hadn't eaten a real meal in weeks, trying to gain some kind of control of the chaos in my had and my life. I had lost about 30 lbs in 3 weeks, and I felt like wanting to disappear into my glass. A few moments after returning from the restroom, without a sense of self or time, I stumbled into the arms of a guy who had probably watched my mission to drink myself into nothingness and was now about to take advantage of the fact that I could not remember my name when he asked. I remember his face and the expression of pity and excitement, I remember realizing immediately that this decision to go with him would haunt me, I remember using him as self punishment. Going home with someone you know will end up hurting you, no matter the scenario, is nothing else than self-hatred materialized.

It does not have to be rape. If you hook up with someone on a regular basis that you are in love with and who does not love you back, and you are aware of your heart being exploited, you are punishing yourself, using the other person as a tool to harm yourself.

When we got to his apartment and I decided I did not want to be there anymore, he took that choice from me and took what he thought was his after paying for the taxi, those were his words before he overwhelmed me. I am pretty tall, long, strong legs, difficult to keep down. But that night, I remember feeling I deserved to be held down, I deserved to be treated like a soulless object, after all he had paid for a taxi I could not afford, and I remember thinking for years after that I had raped myself instead of the guy doing it. I never pressed charges, I was sure I deserved it and I kept in touch with him long after the incidence.

That night I remember running home. In the rain. I had no money for a taxi and even if I could have afforded one, the vision of me would have probably scared the driver to death. I was so drunk I could not focus my pupils anymore, my makeup was running down my face, and I was sobbing so hard I couldn't breathe. I was running for more than two hours through the heavy rain, starting at around 3am in the Western part of Downtown Berlin, arriving on the Eastside at around 530am. I barely stopped, running barefoot through one of the biggest cities in the world, holding my heels in my hand, with not a single coin in my pocket, and a heart that hurt more than my body from what had just happened to me. This couldn't really be me. How did I let myself down like that. How did I fall that deep. Where would I go tomorrow. I just kept running. And I remember having this epiphany of how I had been running from everything I didn't wanna address. That I had been running my entire life, breathlessly from pain to pain without holding on, without really feeling myself, without valuing my breath or standing still to listen to my own voice. I remembered stories of people around me who would get really drunk or use drugs and then would sometimes just start running home. Without a warning. Without an explanation. Running is a symptom of our haunted souls, and while it may be great exercise, it's a bad habit in every other aspect of life.

There are two types of people you see on any given day in any given neighborhood around the world. I call them the walkers and the runners. The runners are people like me. They come in all shapes and sizes, but we all share something in common: We think we have somewhere to be, and fast, and we have no time to look left and right because we have somewhere to go and it's urgent and we will not be satisfied until we arrive. Unfortunately, once we arrive, we realize that the joy of reaching our goal (if experienced at all), is extremely short lived and not sustainable, and that the desiring and the longing and the suffering does not stop. So, we keep running, wondering what it is that we are missing, wondering why we feel so empty and useless when we are doing so much and why we feel so stuck even though we are running so fast.

And then there are the walkers. The walkers are rare and are usually walking at an alarmingly slow pace, usually alone, and more often than not sporting a facial expression that can only be described as… neutral. Calm. Present. When I see them, my anxious self usually gets very impatient, and, depending on my emotional state that day, I might even feel aggravated by the speed with which they are seemingly going nowhere with no sense of urgency. Maybe because I am jealous that they are in no rush, seemingly stress free, not staring at their phones.

Or maybe because they have something I want: the real joy of the journey versus the pipe dream of a destination. Embracing the process without glorifying an end result. Chasing after goals and validations we think will make us happier, richer, prettier, more respected, will always end up exhausting us and taking us away from what it is that we crave: true connection, being fully present, feeling aligned with our senses, feeling alive.

Most people's version of success looks something like this: Get a good job, make the most money possible, gain the highest social status we think we deserve, rinse and repeat and build upon and exceed. Many of us never stop chasing after more and more and more of the same artificial accolades and material things they hope will fill our void. When the answer to the burning question of "What will fulfill me and make me feel whole" will always be: Only the present moment.

"I think everybody should get rich and famous and do everything they ever dreamed of so they can see that it's not the answer." Jim Carey

CHAPTER 4

Healing

My 20s were a blur of unpaid bills, jobs that I quit or got let go from, broken relation and friendships and a carousel of bad decisions leading to more bad decisions. I lived like a runaway. Running from my pain, my fears, my demons. In winter of 2011 I felt like had nothing left to live for. I had spent my entire 20's running and numbing, running from my demons, and numbing my pain with traveling, moving, jumping from job to job, from studies to studies, guy to guy, friendship to friendship. You could call this a fairly typical experience of someone in their 20s that does not know what to do in life. Weirdly enough, I was pretty sure what I wanted from life, I had many talents, hobbies and interests and was passionate about all kinds of experiences. While I was living all this life, working overtime to convince people around me that I was doing fantastic, I had been in severe emotional pain, battling depression, anxiety and eating disorders and keeping it a secret from almost everyone I knew. I can honestly say, and it makes me sad to admit, that I was never really present, never content or at peace, and did not love myself for a single moment throughout all these years. So when my 20's came to an end, I was exhausted. I felt like I had lived at least 50 years of life, numerous lives within that life, in numerous bodies, with countless faces that would hide my shame and self-loathing.

In September of 2011 - I had just spent the past 3 years in a dysfunctional relationship, battling a mix of under eating during the week and binge eating on the weekends - my social anxiety was to the point that I could not go to the post office without sweating so profusely that I was dripping sweat by the time I got to the counter. I could not hold a real job down and would rarely get through a full day at Uni. The only income I had at this point came from selling Cowboy hats on eBay that had been mistakenly delivered to my address and that I lived off for months. My ex had left our tiny shared apartment without a word one day, turned his phone off, moved to a new city and started a new life. He never explained what the breaking point was, he was just gone one day, and he did not have to explain anything. I knew how toxic I had been, for the both of us. Truly loving someone if you hate yourself is next to impossible. After suffering an emotional breakdown, not because my boyfriend had left me, I moved back in with my mom. I was almost 30 years old. No job, no money, no career, no degree, no car, no apartment, nothing in my name.

I had spent the last decade traveling all over the globe, trying to escape whatever was haunting me by pretending, by fake smiling, by boarding planes to places that made me feel like the last person on earth, by sleeping with people that told me how much of a freak I was, how much of an enigma, how exciting and insane I appeared, and how they would never consider keeping me in their lives for good. I understood.

After spending a few months in emotional limbo, New Years eve came and went, and I got extremely sick with the flu and a bad ear infection. My beloved mom wanted me to get a scooter, since I spent hours walking to the little old train station every day and back in the cold. I did not have a car, never owned one, and now lived outside of the city in a small town, next to a little forest and a river that I had never noticed until a couple days later, when it would become somewhat of my second home. 6 days into the Year of 2012, (I remember the day so well since it's my father's birthday) I adopted a Golden Retriever puppy. I went on a website similar to eBay to buy a used motor scooter and instead found a rescue puppy, sitting in the corner of a tiny, dark entry way, staring at me from my computer screen, with big, lonely eyes. They called him Max, and when we drove to pick him up, me in a fever and my mom and I both knowing we were not allowed to own a dog in her small apartment, he sat in that tiny, dark entry way on the 20th floor of a high rise building in a rundown part of East Berlin. The owner said he was sick with an ear infection. And that was that. I carried him down 20 flights of stairs, and I remember feeling completely out of it due to the fever and my own ear infection that impaired my balance. It was one of those dark, dreary Berlin winter days, ice cold but not cold enough to keep the dirty snow from melting and transforming the streets into brown mud slides. From that day on, I would never let go of that dog that saved my life. I called him Elliot, the "light bringer", and that is what he did, he brought light into my life like I had never felt before, and in hindsight he became a messenger foreshadowing my future, foreshadowing that I would have a little boy one day, the love of my life, and that I would call him Lucas Elliot: Double light. Elliot the Golden Retriever puppy, requiring all my attention, loving me unconditionally, became my little savior, my healer, just like it says in the description I had found about his name:

An Elliot will render your dark days with light,

An Elliot will give a selfless comfort to make all things

bright.

He will bring the moon to where the sun lies.

In a heart beat he can turn a sunset into a sun rise.

An Elliot is someone who gives the gift of love,

and from that day onwards he will be your all, beyond and above.

An Elliot will give a strength a hope,

Taking your hand and helping all cope.

An inspiration a muse

Once Elliot touches a heart, it can't ever refuse.

(While I am reading through this cheesy poem, pondering whether to leave it in, Elliot walked through the whole house, making a whole lot of noise on the wood floors, and just jumped onto the couch next to me. I leave it in).

From the moment I had adopted Elliot, my entire life changed. I started completely forgetting about myself, which is a god send for anyone who has ever been consumed by their own shortcomings. I stopped looking into the mirror, and I started spending most of my days outside with my puppy. I adopted Elliot in the deepest, coldest winter, taught him how to fetch in the snow, to listen to his name by playing hide and seek in the forest, and I would lose my shit when he would disappear into the briarwood for a couple rounds of puppy freak outs when we went on our night walks when no soul was out. He was mischievous and would be gone for sometimes 20 minutes at a time, racing through the forest on his own, and I would have a complete meltdown before he would shoot back out of the darkness like a snowflake on speed. I loved that animal more than anything else before, and I am sure people thought I was now completely losing my mind. Elliot learned to swim in the icy river in winter when he was about 4 months old, and in Summer he would chase ducks and we would both swim together in that same river, that was definitely not made for swimming. I did not care, we absolutely loved it. Golden Retrievers shed a lot, so my ritual was to spend hours in nature with him, then give him a bath, then dry , brush him out, before vacuuming the whole appartment, sometimes multiple times a day. I worked a remote job on the weekends from home, and was only gone for a couple of hours each day when I went to university, we were inseparable. Since I did not have a car I carried my growing puppy to the vet that was 2 hours away by foot, sometimes several times a week, if I thought he had a tooth ache or another ear infection, until the vet told me to stop coming. I was broke but would spend any money that I made on dog food, toys, treats. I slept with him, talked to him, and sang lullabies to him. (In fact the first time I realized that Elliot was actually a dog, was the day I brought my human newborn home).

As crazy as all this sounds, pets can play a crucial role in healing from trauma, and in my case, caring for another being, and experiencing unconditional love in that way after years of self abuse, started off a healing journey. Elliot and I would spend most days outside, and I essentially started a year of deep meditation, with myself, often times in isolation and silence, and I finally started listening to my own voice. At first that voice scared me, and was extremely uncomfortable. Sometimes I started singing to myself, or to my dog, or to my unborn son. The song that would make me cry the most was called "Jemand warted auf Dich", (Someone's waiting for you), from the movie "The Rescuers". It is to this day my favorite song and I sing it with my toddler every day, he often sings it to me now which, as you can imagine, is extremely moving and means the world to me. These are the lyrics:

Sei tapfer mein Kind.

Es gibt Menschen, die lieb zu dir sind.

lass die Tränchen und glaube an dich.

jemand wartet auf dich.

nun weine nicht mehr.

ist dir auch heute das Herzchen noch schwer.

morgen lächelst du auch so wie ich!

Jemand wartet auf dich.

Ein Gebet dass du verwahrt hast im Herzen, dass sich schützend vor dich stellt.

bringt dir Freude und das Glück damit deine Welt sich erhellt.

verzage nur nicht eine schönere Welt ist in Sicht.

Drum sei tapfer und glaube an dich.

Jemand wartet schon auf dich!

Be brave, little one

Make a wish for each sad little tear

Hold your head up though no one is near

Someone's waiting for you

Don't cry, little one

There'll be a smile where a frown use to be

You'll be part of the love that you see

Someone's waiting for you

Always keep a little prayer in your pocket

And you're sure to see the light

Soon there'll be joy and happiness

And your little world will be bright

Have faith, little one

'Til your hopes and your wishes come true

You must try to be brave, little one

Someone's waiting to love you

So imagine me, walking through the forest, over fields, singing this song, crying, feeling all these years, going through all these emotions that would come to the surface by being on my own, with nothing ahead of me, I was fully present, maybe for the first time in my life. I saw seasons change before my eyes, I started appreciating being alone, watching snow melt, running through corn mazes for hours without meeting anyone, watching my dog jump into his beloved river with such joy that I was laughing out loud. On one of our hikes I found a dead tree. It was this one lonely, black, dead tree skeleton in the middle of nowhere, that was sticking out like a soar thumb in the middle of dead grass, and it looked so sad and lonely, it reminded me of myself. I took pictures of it in every season, at every time of day, in the early morning, during a snow storm, during sunset, in spring when everything around it was blooming. Its surroundings were beautiful but the tree itself never changed, it stayed black and dead. Over the course of that year that I spent in the wilderness with Elliot, I slowly stopped visiting that tree, I stopped seeing myself in that tree, and I stopped crying at its feet. That tree was not me. I would not stay dead and alone, I could feel myself healing.

At numerous points in my 20s I was what you would consider completely broke. I never really saw it that way since not having money had been such a normal state for me ever since I left home at almost 17. My focus was never on money, and I only really paid attention to it when I was so broke that I could not afford my bus ticket and had to do what you call "Schwarzfahren" in German, taking public transport without paying for it, hoping the ticket inspectors would not catch you. They did catch me countless times, a highly embarrassing situation to find yourself in, and I always tried to argue myself out of it, either using a different language claiming I would not understand the ticket machines, acting that this was an emergency and I had to urgently go somewhere and forgot to pay. Sometimes that actually worked, but many times it would not and I was fined. I was a liar, an actor, a scammer, a con-artist. I did not take responsibility for my actions and never learned from my mistakes. Instead of always making sure to have enough money to buy a ticket to not get into another compromising sitatution, I took the risk of getting caught, for years, countless times, for a decade.

If you never take responsibility for your mistakes, you start disrespecting yourself more than anyone else ever could, and this disrespect will inform everything you do, every relationship you enter, every job you do, every thought you think. You will identify as untrustworthy, as a fraud, as a loser. I know I did. So you keep on disrespecting yourself until you find yourself going home with a guy you know has bad intentions, maybe because you crave to feel physical pain that matches your inner pain, or because you feel you deserve to be punished for your flaws, or simply because you feel that you are finally about to be really seen if someone just mistreats you enough. Writing this I wonder about stigma. Will you, dear reader, judge me until the day we die for opening up like this? Will this be my new identity, the girl that got raped and thought she deserved it? Maybe. But I am not writing this to tell you something about me and I am not worried about image or persona.

My story belongs to you now, to everyone reading this, to everyone suffering right now, to a world that is in pain. I am writing this to reach someone who has been where I have been, and if that is you, I wanna look at you and tell you: It is NOT your fault, you do NOT deserve this, and your pain is not who you are, you did not choose or cause this pain. I wanna tell you that I am with you in this, that I am not better, worse, not stronger or weaker. We are equals, human, vulnerable, flawed, fallible, and we both deserve to accept and love ourselves, no matter what. This self hatred is an illusion created out of a toxic cocktail of genetics, upbringing, trauma, and bad luck. Your identity does not exist, it is an illusion that you have invented, to cope, to get by, to punish yourself. It is an illusion you can let go in any moment. In this very moment you are allowed to release it, you are allowed to stop hurting yourself.

CHAPTER 5

The Pursuit of Purpose

I am convinced it is impossible for us human beings to be content without having some sense of purpose. The problem is that we confuse purpose with something outside of us, something greater than ourselves that we need to strive for and work hard on.

I believe that everyone is born with their purpose built in, and that it is the exact opposite of what the self-help industry wants to sell us: Something grandiose, some divine concept, some extraordinary secret that has to be unlocked. We are taught a sense of "what we should be aiming for" from a very young age on. You learn certain subjects in school, without being able to explore what it really is that moves and inspires you, your parents might have a few ideas for your future and the internet with its endless, completely unfathomable possibilities that are seemingly waiting for us, makes it extremely difficult to figure out what we really love and want to focus on. I don't think social media made the problem of us not being able to listen to our instincts worse, it is simply mirroring back the insanity that is our society: You can be anything you want, and it is your responsibility to reach your full potential, and then some.

To me, purpose can be small, quiet, simple. The problem is, that all the options that we are confronted with daily - I call it the toxic noise - are too loud and constantly interrupt the voice within us, the one that tells us what it is we truly love to do, that gives us a sense of belonging and service, a sense of being enough.

For some people, purpose simply means they grow and keep a beautiful rose garden. Do you know these kinds of people? Tending to their flowers, talking about nothing else, always with a smile and a strange peace around them, an aura of stillness. For people like me, and maybe you, those peaceful purposefully still people were always very suspect to me. I almost feared them because I didn't understand. I mistrusted how satisfied they seemed and how content with so little. The secret lies in not needing more: People who listen to their instincts instead of societal norms, family members, religion, culture, and simply stick to what makes them feel at peace, live in exactly the harmony we, the seekers, are longing for. Finding and moving in a space that combines passion and potential but lacks pressure and pain, leads to ultimate inner peace.

The times I truly feel at peace are moments spent with my son. Moments where nothing else matters than his beating heart, his breath when he is sleeping, his adoring eyes I can see all the love in the world in, his tiny fingers closing around my thumb, his soft feet in my hands, me feeding him, me watching him sleep, trying to stay awake and able to cater to his every need since his life was now and forever from this moment on way more important than my own. There is nothing else to do than to love this soul that now walks outside of my body and being loved back with a fierceness and a resilience that takes my breath away. The love of a mother is the perfect example of purpose: it feels completely natural, instinctive, inexplicable, there is no force, it doesn't demand respect or celebration, it is not loud, it doesn't need accolades, it just is.

I am not religious, and I don't believe in an afterlife, however, I do believe that energies survive after physical death and that we live in a constant chaos of the energies our ancestors left us with. I do believe that we all have a purpose on this planet, or in this simulation, or whatever it is that you believe we find ourselves in, and to me this purpose is not to prepare for paradise or to behave well enough to go to heaven, or to get ready for some kind of judgement day - instead I strongly believe that our purpose is to limit our own suffering and the suffering of others during our life time and to find moments of peace and cultivate them as much as possible to find joy and meaning in our existence.

Happiness however, the entity that everyone is after, and whose pursuit is subject of countless self-help books, seems to me the wrong goal. And I tell you why.

Happiness is not a state. And it's not a destination. The pleasure of a happy moment subsides way faster than the agony of a painful one. Happiness is only felt in fleeting flashes of consciousness, in short moments of the realization that you feel happy. Have you ever noticed how the reward for something you were fighting for or working towards never or rarely feels as satisfying as you had anticipated? For people like me, and friends of mine with strong imposter syndrome (feelings of inadequacy that persist despite evident success. 'Imposters' suffer from chronic self-doubt and a sense of intellectual fraudulence that override any feelings of success or external proof of their competence), struggling to experience satisfaction after accomplishing a goal we thought is crucial to our happiness, can lead to more suffering.

So, if you make happiness your goal, you are constantly striving and chasing something that will a) not end your suffering, b) not feel as good as you thought it would, making you yearn for more and c) will not be sustainable.

In the hunt for happiness, you will find yourself in a constant chase for thrills, nothing will ever satisfy you and you might become obsessed with experiencing Highs, getting addicted to things that provide instant gratification, such as shopping, sex, food, drugs, but what you will not achieve, is inner peace.

I am convinced that many people who are desperately trying to find their purpose end up in caregiving jobs. Doing something for others without expecting anything in return is the truest form of purpose and can bring immediate peace to a suffering soul. Nowadays, I am trying to find a balance (terrible word) between my life as a mom and work, I always feel torn between the two things that I feel are my calling: Being a mother and helping people transform their lives. I sometimes dream of not having any other ambitions and just fully indulging in the sweet and fleeting moments of childhood without feeling the need to fulfill my own desires of a career of passion. But I do know that there is a time and place for inner peace, and I know where I can find it.

When I was in the midst of starting to work after being home with my son for his first three years, I felt all the pressure in the world on my shoulders of fulfilling my potential, as a woman, a mom, an entrepreneur, a human and at the same time feeling an immense amount of guilt not being completely and utterly content with just being a mother.

I wrote an article back then and I called it

The Lethal P's

"Lately I've been feeling something I can only describe as torn apart. For no special reason, life seems extraordinarily overwhelming and chaotic at present when in reality, nothing has changed, and everything is running smoothly and consistently on the outside. No tidal waves, no earthquakes, not even a big storm. To be honest, my life has never had this much built in routine and structure - something I never allowed to form but always envisioned would offer an immense amount of peace and purpose. And there it is, that bad, bad word. Purpose. In all this brain and gut salad that I am gnawing on at the moment, the common cure I am relentlessly fantasizing about is A, My, The purpose.

In order to create my neurotic version of consecutive successful days, weeks, projects, months, years, relationships, I am hunting down a different purpose on any given day to satisfy any given desire, silence any given doubts, heal any given wounds. Chasing this ever enticing concept of fulfillment, of finally feeling whole, of reaching my - wait for it - full potential. Another one of those hell-ish P words. So much has been written about this abstract monster, and while I am now here writing this, it becomes clear to me that it is sitting on my shoulder, looming over me like a self-fulfilling prophecy: don't acknowledge it or it will come true. Don't admit to yourself that you feel unaccomplished, or the house of cards you built with the blood, sweat and tears of your broken dreams and aspirations will crash and burn once and for all and you will have to show the world and worse, yourself, that this is all there is: a big pile of dust that was once your potential.

"But who gets to decide my potential?" yells that rebellious 16-year-old in me that seems to still question (and make?) at least 75% of all my life decisions. Who decides what it is that will make me an ultimate success? Is it my alcoholic

German teacher, who told me I needed to become a published author, my failed drama teacher who urged me to audition at a renowned acting school (I failed miserably), is It my mom who never gets tired of reminding me that I don't live up to my full potential but never elaborates on what exactly that would look like? Or was my dad right when he tried to convince me from the moment I could understand him that I would fail in each and every of my poor endeavors and would never reach any kind of success with my specific disposition?

Is it the world around me that seems to value nothing more than a perfected exterior and a never specified amount of material items that say: I made it, I am richer/happier/better than you? Or it my son who believes the height of my potential would be to build a Lego tower on the floor with him, which I, the hunter and gatherer of purpose and potential, rarely ever gets around to these days. And this is where my heart sinks and my momguilt overshadows any logical reasoning and the world spins and I can't seem to find a beginning or end to the day or the day after today. Because there it is, that third lethal word that starts with P, that seems to weigh most if not all of us down: Pressure. Pressure to not only perfectly perform every role we chose for ourselves, and every part society sees us in.

I realize that I may never find my purpose, that I will always fall short on expectations, may it be my own or others', but what I do know is that Peace, that really good word with P, only exists in moments for me. Peace to me is not a state, it's not a goal, not a plan, it's not forcible and can't be aspired to. It happens when I let go and don't strive for anything, when I stop trying, when I don't do more but way less, when I don't run but sit down, next to my child, who wants nothing more than me present, not moving, just there. When I stop the planning and debating and discussing and strategizing, but instead bear my silence and listen and stop questioning. When I stay still amidst my raging thoughts and let them exhaust themselves and instead of furiously searching for an answer to one of my million questions, accept that I don't have the answers. And that I don't need any, not in this moment."

CHAPTER 6

How to Forgive Yourself

I know that women who felt rejected by their fathers struggle with self esteem and a warped image of their femininity and self worth, especially regarding the other gender. But I cannot blame my father for the life I lived. The little girl that came into this world was hypersensitive, deeply introverted, psychic to the point of scaring herself (I can sense when people are pregnant across oceans before they know they are, I can feel earthquakes coming, I can sense deaths of people that I don't know and never met from continents away. I will dream of things and they happen the next day. This "gift" is something I did not share with many people, and it was unsettling, especially for a kid that struggles to fit in, into her own family, into her own perceptions of herself.)

Toxic positivity

This next part might trigger you, so please be careful while you continue reading this: If I would have to draw my inner self it would resemble a monster, a mixture of a devil looking creature that has pain and self loathing written all over its face. I would still draw myself like that today, even in my happiest moments. I came to the conclusion that the monster I see inside myself is not me, nor my soul, but that I am in fact drawing and mirroring a darkness that lives in all of us, and since I feel it so deeply and connect with it so strongly, I am a walking mirror of the underworld we all have within us. I project the depth of the human experience that I witness in others and relate to it to understand it, to understand the world as a whole, the other side of the sun.

As a child, these emotions are confusing and can lead to immense amounts of shame. Today I can live with the fact that people see me and describe me in a way that is completely opposite of my self image. Please note, that I don't subscribe to what therapists would tell me about having to work to change that self image. Not everything inside you that seems dark has to be eradicated to live a fulfilled life. Your self is a construct, an illusion that you create to make sense of your desires, your struggles, and to cope with the world around you. There is no real self, there is only your perception and how it influences your human experience. To end your suffering, you don't have to change yourself, but simply have to become aware of negative or destructive thoughts, and release them or work through them. You can also embrace and accept them, and for me this means finding a creative outlet to let it breathe. Expressing myself through writing is a direct consequence of my darkness. Hence why I was avoiding it for so long.

Darkness is part of the world, part of ourselves, and fearing it and running from it or trying to eliminate it will lead to more self loathing, since it cannot be eliminated. I realize now that the ugliness I see when I look at my face is not my inner or outer appearance, but simply a part of the world that I feel connected to and that I wanna heal in others. It leads me to a special creativity I would not be able to share otherwise.

This connection to darkness is my gift. Like a dog that can smell cancer, I can feel pain, and that's what I see in my eyes. Without judging it. I can remove myself now, my ego, my so-called identity from it and just view me as a vessel, as someone who is so familiar and comfortable in pain, that he has the chance to heal it in others. Does this sound crazy to you? Chances are, if you picked up this book, you can relate. I am not here to scare you, but I want you to acknowledge and accept what it is that causes your suffering to then be able to release it. I made this promise to myself, that, if I would ever expose myself like this, and write about the other side of my soul, that I would go as deep as I have to to grasp the truth, to be as honest as I can possibly be, and to explain everything as graphically as possible, so that you can follow me down here and we can both heal.

CHAPTER 7

How to Re-unite With Your Body

After I started slowly healing from the inside, and a peace set in that I had not felt before in that way, I suddenly started becoming more mindful of what I would eat. When you grow up and you are being told that your body is ugly, misshapen and unattractive, this will stay your default connection with it until you actively work on changing your relationship with your body in order to respect it.

To this day I suffer from body dysmorphia, but I now know that this is in fact a disorder and that my brain distorts my self image. I now listen to family and friends that love me, and I believe them: Just because your eyes cannot see something, does not mean it is not true. I have reached a point in my life, maybe it's age, or maybe I am just sick of my own bullshit, where I don't care about being in perfect shape anymore and I am sometimes shocked how happy and peaceful this feels. Feeling good in my body with all its imperfections is so strange and new to me, and it opens up so many possibilities and frees up so much of my time. You get addicted to suffering, your disorder is an addiction and you might feel naked and scared without it. For me, controlling my eating has always been a coping mechanism, I would restrict my food intake to the point of going weeks by only drinking water and coffee and chewing gum, without ever feeling hungry, only to then binge on junk food for a week and the cycle would start up again. The bizarre part was, that it was never really about the way I looked, but more about the false sense of control that especially not eating for long periods of time would grant me. Nowadays this state of mind seems very far away, of course I still have days where my jeans feel tight and I could definitely work out more and eat healthier. But food does not play a big role in my life anymore, I replaced this obsession with other, way more meaningful things, I embrace all the curves and soft parts that were not there before I had a baby, and I feel sexier than ever. Being comfortable and in sync with your body has little to do with what you actually look like, and everything to do with how you treat yourself and how you talk to yourself. Working out has been a huge part on this journey to a healed mind and soul, but as someone who used to obsess with weight, I am mindful of not making it the center of my every day anymore. For me personally, a healthy mind and body is created through treating yourself in a respectful and compassionate way, starving yourself or over exercising is the opposite of self respect, and if you have a history of eating disorders, I would always be mindful of overdoing it.

I mainly follow a Vegan diet now and embracing that played a huge part in my healing from the inside out, if was truly life changing and I strongly believe that being in tune with your surroundings and other living and breathing creatures and being conscious of what you consume and act responsibly and aware of the connection you have with the universe, will give you the best results when it comes to your physical and mental health. I am a strong believer that you can heal most of your bodily ailments by cleaning up your diet, eliminating dairy altogether (please read the "China Study" or watch the documentrary "Earthlings," narrated by Joaquin Phoenix to learn more).

Advocating a Vegan diet has nothing to do with wanting to tell you what to eat, but trying to convey the message of mindful and conscious living. I heard this wonderful story the other day watching an interview that Joaquin Phoenix gave to his two sisters Summer and Rain on their podcast. They were talking about a distinct and very moving moment when their whole family suddenly adopted a Vegan lifestyle. Joaquin and his sister were very young when they saw how an animal was slaughtered and came running to their mother, devastated, crying, in disbelief how she had failed to tell them about the origins of the hot dogs and burgers on their table. Accusing her of withholding that crucial information of how animals had to suffer and die for the food they were eating. The children were inconsolable. Joaquin and his sisters remembered how her mother started crying, fully responsive and open to the pain and compassion of her children, and how from that day on, a moment over 30 years ago, their parents and all 5 children became Vegan and never looked back. This tale of compassion and how innocent, pure love of the hearts of children touched and influenced the path of a whole family for the simple fact that the adults listened and understood, is stunning and I wish the entire world would work in that way.

It does not and I understand that. I also understand that food is an incredibly personal topic and I was absolutely questioning if I should include it in this book. However, if we talk about all around healing and health I cannot deny you the truth and if there is just one person out there that considers to stop consuming animals and animal products after reading this, or goes on to explore the topic further, it was worth risking to lose some of you here.

As a spiritual being that feels energies clearly and is highly influenced by them, eating animal products has palpable and immediate negative effects on my mood, my health, my mindset. If you wanna eliminate suffering within yourself, causing other beings to suffer feels counter intuitive. I have and always had a deep connection with animals, and if you have ever spent time around cows or pigs, chances are you might fall in love with their sensitivity and develop love and compassion. Slaughtering them for consumption, or drinking milk that was meant for their offspring that will die for it, will cause me to break out in cystic acne and gain unhealthy weight. When I stopped eating dairy years ago, my skin that was covered in volcanic looking acne from coming off years on birth control pills (highly toxic) and a poor diet, cleared up within a few months and completely transformed. If you struggle with digestive issues, cut out dairy and meat for a few weeks, you might see results after a few days. I have never met someone who follows a plant based diet that suffers from IBS, to be honest I did not even know that condition existed before moving to the United States, where fast food and processed meat is part of people's every day diet.

However, loving your body, especially after a history of abuse, means you need to listen to what feels good for you, not for me, not for any fitness guru on Instagram, but for you. You need to start with love, and go from there. And I know this sounds crazy for us who don't really know how self love feels, but you gotta fake it til you make it: treat your body as if you would truly love and cherish it, and it will repay you and heal you and you will both thrive together.

CHAPTER 8

How to be Free

I was almost 30 years old and had to hold a presentation on the language of the Maori, the indigenous Polynesian people of New Zealand. My ambitious idea was to teach the class the Maori alphabet. Due to my anxiety I had cared more about what I would wear that day (I had developed a hyperhydrosis disorder at the highest point of my anxiety and depression that I explained with all kinds of other problems, like not leaving the house for weeks, my social anxiety, my eating disorder, temperature changes, medications I would take. Unfortunately the day of the presentation turned out to be an extremely hot summer's day. As soon I started to speak in front of the class, my hands immediately started sweating so much that I had large, salty water stains on my notes and was at one point unable to read the running ink. I had sweat through my pair of dark blue jeans and could feel my chuck taylors filling up with water. The more I started sweating the more I would sweat, the salty water was running down my forehead, my back, making my light, flow top stick to my spine, my hair stuck to the sides of my head and my eyes started burning from the salt running into it.

In the middle of one of the most humiliating moments of my life, something occurred to me: There was nothing left to protect. I was humiliated to the bone. My teacher knew it, the students (who were mostly around 10 to 12 years younger than me) knew it, we all knew it: and we were all caught in this extreme discomfort of my anxiety. Then something happened that I will never forget: I was humbled. My ego left me, my identity vanished: Whatever I had tried to portray to that teacher or the students in that class over the course of the past year, clearly a facade of confidence, had just been debunked, my scam was uncovered, I was exposed. I never felt more vulnerable, more naked. And suddenly this indescribable freedom set in. There seemed to be nothing left of me, and thus, I was finally fully present, fully in the room, fully in the moment, fully in that class with everyone else, I was clearly alive shown by all my bodily functions, and that was all I was. Alive, but without self. And I slowly stopped producing more sweat, the old sweat got cold, my anxiety calmed down until it was fully vanished, and my voice slowly got slower and firmer, and softer, And my heart started slowing down, and I looked up and down and I was there. This was my body in that moment, this was the voice I was using, whatever that me was did not matter. I had never felt this free.

Vulnerability will set you free like nothing else. Let it destroy you, share it and it will set you free.

CHAPTER 9

Fear and Failure

There are two experiences that disguise themselves as your enemies, that will build your resilience, wisdom and confidence in yourself more than anything else, they are called: Fear and Failure.

Fear is what you have to walk towards, allowing the chance of failure, and by overcoming and enduring both, over and over again, every day, you will build up resistance so strong that these two daunting emotions will become your best friends.

Let's start with fear. Fear is not only helpful in keeping us alive, but it is also a great guide when it comes to our true desires. Obviously, we are afraid of actual dangerous things, but more often than not we tend to be scared of something that is inevitable for our development, empowerment and fulfillment: Change. Change is one of my favorite subjects as I tend to be constantly changing and transforming in my own life and it is one of the things I feel extremely comfortable in and that has enriched the way I live and think and feel in so many ways that I believe that walking towards change instead of fearing it will improve your life in every way possible and can actually end your emotional suffering if you overcome it.

Fear of change is the equivalent of a cage you have the key to but refuse to use it.

Let's say you struggle with losing weight. Why do so many people wanna lose weight but some of them never will and others do, what is the difference? Let us assume that the same two people have the same desire to lose weight and suffer from the same amount of emotional pain brought on by their weight. Why does one lose the weight and the other doesn't?

Because desire and pain are not enough to achieve a goal.

Other components play a role, such as 1) Discipline 3) Circumstances 4) Genetics. I am, however, a firm believer that you can manipulate all of these factors greatly, if you confront and overcome your fear of failure, and I believe that 90% of people would go through all the hard grind of weight loss, if there was a guarantee that they could not fail. The reason why you don"t start is the same reason why you give up over and over again: Your Fear of Failure. Overcoming a fear is in my experience only possible by confronting it head on: every time you are scared to do something (non life threatening, we are talking about things you desire and you would wanna take on if you were not afraid), you make the conscious decision to go for it. You will find that the sheer act of doing something you were scared of, will give you a rush and a feeling of power that is unlike no other, and it will unleash confidence in your own abilities that are unmatched and that you cannot set free by staying in your comfort zone, paralyzed by self induced fear. You will also encounter an entity that you tried to avoid all this time: Failure.

Failure is the consequence of you "going for it". If you would not have overcome the fear of starting, you would not have been able to fail. It will be a new experience that you should cherish and be immensely proud of. Getting over failure, acknowledging that it happened, NOT letting it discourage you and not giving up despite it, will give you a sense of pride that easy success will never give you! In fact, I strongly believe that the real joy does not lie in reaching the top of the mountain, but in the pride of getting up after stumbling, almost breaking your leg and still-continuing to climb.

How to Get Shit Done

Perfectionism

All my life I had people pass me by and achieve goals that, so I was told, would have been easy for me to achieve, and yet I did not reach any of them. In school, I was told by teachers that I was smart, that I could write, and as I got older terms like "talented", "beautiful", "attractive", "special" got thrown at me. I did not relate to any of these things, but that was not what caused me to fail. What caused me to fail was my perfectionism. Let me explain:

I knew that some things came easy to me and that some things felt unattainable. Writing for example felt incredibly easy but being popular or having the perfect body would never be in the cards for me. Over the course of my adolescent years, caught up in all my insecurities, I watched girls that were seemingly average looking date the hottest guys. Or people with rather boring personalities become extremely popular, or people that were not more intelligent or talented than others get the best jobs and the highest grades. I talked to some of my friends about this and it's very common amongst highly insecure people (women especially seem prone to this) to ruin opportunities, years of their lives, or at least their mood with their toxic perfectionism.

I do not think the devil exists but if it would, my personal devil is called Perfectionism. I fight it nowadays with every fibre of my being, but it is and will stay an ever present battle in my life, every day and in everything I do, no matter if I am writing a book, raising my son or simply straightening my hair: This fucking devil sits on my shoulder and tries to keep me from starting things, doing things, finishing things, loving things, trusting things, loving myself, getting shit done. And my number one focus nowadays, is to get shit done. Getting shit done is the opposite of feeling stuck, it's moving, forward, sideways, but at least it is moving and what I have learned is: Every movement, every action counts on the way out of depression. Movement is the opposite of depression. Perfectionism however, is this evil creature that wants to keep you stuck, it is your number one opponent on the way out of paralysis and into empowerment. Doing something sloppily, and trust me I had to learn this the hard way, is always better than not doing it at all. You will learn that sloppy might not get you anywhere and that will be a lesson. You will try again. But you are not stuck, you are evolving.

The reason for your perfectionism is your fear of failure and you not feeling enough. You are acting out of fear, not out of love. Just going for something, without knowing the outcome, without knowing for certain that you are capable of doing it, takes a lot love for yourself. You would have to grant yourself the try, the failure. I know of course, that coming from a place of self love is very difficult for many of us, so you might ask: How will I ever get over being a perfectionist if I have to love myself first? Well, you don't. You simply turn the chronology around (I do it every day, it works): You start doing things without the goal of doing it perfectly, which might by the way seem really rebellious and exciting to you, as it will open so many doors that seemed closed, so enjoy the ride! And if you continue down this road of routinely laying the focus on doing things, instead of perfecting them, life will become a lot fuller, and it will move in way more directions.

Imagine a river that you desperately try to straighten out. A river will never be completely straight unless it is artificial, flowing through steel or plastic. The same applies to your life. Desperate attempts of keeping your little river in line and perfectly straight will leave you feeling empty and unfulfilled, you don't let any other influences into your life, no new ideas, no adventure, nothing will lead you to new shores. When you, however, build new river junctions, new fish will swim into your imperfect river, waters will mix, and you will create a whole new eco system, new life! You might go down some wild waters on your journey and end up floating around in the wrong direction or crashing down a waterfall, but you also have countless chances of ending up where you were meant to go all along, and encountering people and moments that will enrich your life.

Don't deny yourself the chance to life a full life by trying to perfect it. Don't deny others to love you because you don't ever show them the real you. And don't deny yourself your own love, that you are worthy of with and especially because of all the beautiful imperfections that make you beautiful and special.

CHAPTER 11

How to Get What You Want

The Truth about Manifestation

I am sure by now you are as sick of the word as I am. Manifestation is a concept that can easily be misrepresented and misused, scamming people into thinking if they pin a picture of a yacht on their fridge, a big boat will magically appear and they will need to go buy an anchor.

Manifesting works like this: There are things in your life, that are already yours, that have already been instilled in you from the day you were born: Those are things you naturally love and that love you back with ease, things and people and energies that are meant for you, that you not only desire but that also draw you to them like magnets and vice versa. These are things that feel effortless, people you love from the moment you meet them, things that make you feel at home, calm, no effort needed at all to imagine them, no chase needed to make them see you. Manifesting is nothing more or less than listening to your intuition, and as hard as that might be with all the noise around us, it is not a magic trick (but the outcome will feel magical). I would also argue that it's not a foreign concept to you at all, you are doing it every day with things that seem to magically fall into place. The trick to listening to your intuition and let it work for you and lead you, is to stop judging that inner voice, and to stop questioning its intentions. The biggest part in that are outside forces. If you have parents that tell you to live against your intuition, don't listen. And if you have friends that judge you following your heart, you need new friends. Things that are not meant for you, will feel painful to achieve. You can go after them, chase them, wrestle with them, but you will never fully enjoy them and they will never fulfill you, end suffering within you, or bring true joy or peace. If they instead fill you with joyful anticipation, a sense of reformation, transformation, elevation, some would say a higher power lifting your spirits naturally, then this is your intuition calling you, telling you which way to go. Being oversensitive, highly emotional and intuitive might seem like a difficult combination for some people, but if you allow yourself to truly be that and embrace this disposition in you, you can have whatever it is that you truly desire, because you inner voice is louder than in others. Being a tad delusional (I call it innovative) might serve you well especially if you have loud inner and outer critics: believing something that is not there yet, that you have to build first, surrounded by people that don't believe in you, is like inventing the wheel when no-one knows what driving is yet. Choosing a path that you can only feel, that your eyes cannot see yet, is the highest form of rebellion, and people will come at you trying to sway you from it, no-one likes when people change and think outside of their box, it makes them uncomfortable. The mind spaces that will be created by you and only you, are manifestations of your purpose, and if you don't listen to them and go after them with confidence and irrevocable persistence, they will stay lost in the universe, unmaterialized, when they could have become your legacy, as they belonged to you and only you and were only able to form by and through you. The world needs you to fulfill your true purpose, don't deny the universe and yourself the chance to see and benefit from all your fantastic creations.

Let me give you an example of what manifestation looks like in action: In 2007 after I had completed 2 years of trade school to become a foreign language clerk, my goal was to complete an internship in the US to go work as a secretary of a diplomat. As a kid I spent almost every Summer in Florida and America had always felt like a place of abundance and freedom that I was missing in cold, uptight Germany (please don't come for me, fellow Germans, just be happy I am gone haha). People seemed friendlier, looser, they greeted you exuberantly without knowing you (I to this day like superficial friendliness amongst strangers better than authentic rudeness, I, again, apologize to all German readers, not everything is bad over there, but I spent 30 winters in Berlin, I deserve to rant a little). From an early age on I loved the United States and people along the way always told me how I would end up living here one day, which always took me by surprise. I never planned to move to the US, especially because immigration is extremely complicated, but I must have somewhere in the back of my mind established that one day in the future this would be home. In Summer 2007 I sat on a couch at a new friend's house in Garden Grove, California, 5,790 miles from home, and fell in love with my future husband and father of my son. It took about 3 seconds to fall hopelessly in love with him, and I don't care what you have heard - it happened to me, so it can happen. He came through the door and I sat on the couch and we both felt something that can only be described as two powerful magnets pulling towards each other, and we had not even spoken yet. After 3 months together I had to leave and fly home, devastated and heartbroken, certain I would never see this guy again that I fell so deeply in love with. Jon however was not heartbroken or devastated at all and I remember that hurt me even more. He let me go with the words: " I know we will see each other again, this isn't our time, this is not Goodbye but see you soon." Imagine my heart crumbling as I left to board my plane, I cried the whole flight home, around 11 hours, behind big sunglasses. It would take 6 years apart from each other and a lot of life experiences later, that I would understand what he had meant. He had manifested us being together forever from the moment we met, and all he did from the day I left was working on the details. He checked in on me every couple of months via email, and was often disappointed at how cynical about life and love I had become after leaving him, but he never stopped contact, no matter how dismissive I got. We both went through several relationships, jobs, successes, failures. And 6 years later, in the fall of 2012, when I had moved back in with my mother and was a new mom to my Golden Retriever puppy, we started talking regularly. I was finally healing and taking care of my inner needs, and could finally allow this guy who I had been madly in love with and had felt a spiritual connection with like I had with nobody else before or after, I could finally open up and hear his words: We are meant for each other, I will love you, you will love me, I wanna take care of you, I want you to take care of me, bring your puppy, stay with me, let's be a family. I must admit, I thought he had lost his mind. I thought he was cocky and weird and his firmness and trust in our connection and his inexhaustible affection for me scared the heck out of me. What he did was nothing short of manifesting something he already knew existed in the future: US. Our family. Our love. Our future. Someone that is that sure of something can scare the heck out of people who don't listen to their intuition. And I hadn't listen to mine in years. I had given up on my dream of moving to the United States, long ago, and had instead listened to many voices telling me to stop being delusional and start following the rules. And I had been miserable. I remember asking him for years after we were already parents and married, WHY he was so sure that we belonged together and that we would actually make it, against the odds of me living across the ocean and living a completely different life that I never considered sharing with him. All he ever answered was: "I believed in our connection, what we had was special, our chemistry was meant to be." Always the same answer. And when I ask him today what his plan B would have been if I had said No to his crazy ideas: "No Plan B. I was sure." Now if my husband would be like me, a dreamer, slightly delusional at times, a little irrational or prone to dramatic behavior, his devotion and conviction would have seemed to make more sense to me and others around. But my husband is the exact opposite of all that: he is rational, logical, reasonable, analytical. The fact that he was 100% sure that we would be a family seemed like a miracle to me and people around us, and there we have it: that is exactly what following your true intuition feels like: If you listen to your true purpose, no matter what it is that draws you to it, things will shift in a way in your favor that you will suddenly feel like the universe is working for you. By listening to his gut feeling of me being right for him and him being right for me, my future husband created a whole world that would be ours in the future, without him being aware of it, without a masterplan, all he had was a heart he listened to.

CHAPTER 12

How to Have it All

Look around you

Breathe

Are you in immediate danger?

Are you cold?

Can you feel your heartbeat?

Any pain in your body?

Do you have food in the fridge?

If you get thirsty, will there be water to drink?

A bed with a pillow when you get tired?

Are your children sleeping peacefully?

Is your dog by your feet?

Who do you miss in this moment?

If you wanna go for a walk, will your feet carry you?

Will the street you are walking on be safe enough?

Breathe

Notice your breath

Focus on where the air enters your nose

Feel where the air lets your body rise

Is it your chest?

Your stomach?

Come back to your breath

When thoughts carry you away

And away again

Don't fight it

Just notice it and let it go

You are still here.

Still breathing

Conscious

Alive

A body full of warmth

A beating heart

Working lungs

Some ailments

Many wounds

Scars

But notice that you are still here.

Go back to your breath and notice

How there is nothing else to do in this moment

No need to flee

No need to plan

Let it go

And ask yourself

How many people would give everything to be
where you are right now

How many people that you know of

And then think of the millions of people you
will never meet

that would instantly switch lives with you

Look around

What do you see

Is this life that you live worth living?

And if it is not, is there still something you can
be grateful for in this moment?

Anything?

And if there is nothing, what decision can you make in this moment

To make a change

Focus on this decision for a moment

Breathe

Let's focus on what that change would mean for your life

Breathe

Look around

Is this life worth making this small change?

A small change that could lead to another small change

That could lead to a bigger change

What would make life worth living again?

Or is your breath enough for now

In this moment

Is this life worth making a small decision

For change

Breathe

Focus on your breath

Can you make the decision?

I am rooting for you

All the way to all the change you need

But until we are there

I am grateful for your lungs

That help you breathe

For your brain, that tries so hard

To focus on the air filling them.

Vanessa was born in Berlin, Germany. With the goal to become an interpreter for the UN, she attended trade school and graduated as a Foreign Language Correspondent in Spanish and English, before going on to study English and German linguistics at University of Excellence "Freie Universität of Berlin". After moving out at the age of 17, she worked as a model, actress, translator and tutor; which afforded her to travel all over the world while attending university. Vanessa has appeared in movies like "Aeon Flux" with Charlize Theron, music videos, German movies and TV shows. After internships at PR and media companies, she went to an interview for one of the most sought after TV internships on European television at RTL Exclusiv (German equivalent of E! news). She got hired on the spot and did her first interview only a few hours later with Formula 1 driver Lewis Hamilton and went to cover many movie junkets, red carpet events, Berlin Fashion Week and Berlinale, the German Oscars. With only a student contract and very little pay, she interviewed Superstars like Leonardo DiCaprio, Robert Downey Jr., Sir Ben Kingsley, Penelope Cruz, Salma Hayek, Kevin James, Rachel MacAdams, Guy Richie and many many more, working day and night. After suffering a severe burnout she quit her dream job and after many ups and downs immigrated to the US (California), with only a suitcase and her Golden Retriever Elliot. Being a survivor of childhood trauma and suffering from depression and eating disorders for 30 years, she finally went on a healing journey. After losing 90lbs after having her son in 2015 she started sharing her life and struggles online and gained a following as an inspiring figure, and motivational speaker and life coach. She started her podcast "Vanessa's Voices" where she showcases stories of inspiring thought leaders, entrepreneurs, mental health professionals and survivors and finally finished her book: "Depressed to Success." Her goal is to raise awareness for mental health, to relief suffering, empower female entrepreneurs and people all over the world to live a life of fulfillment and inner peace.